CHESTER

A Portrait in Old Picture Postcards

by
Karlyn Goulborn and Gillian Jackson

S. B. Publications
1987

First published in 1987 by S. B. Publications.

5 Queen Margaret's Road, Loggerheads, Nr. Market Drayton, Shropshire, TF9 4EP.

© Copyright S. B. Publications 1987.

ISBN 1 870708 02 4

Printed in Great Britain by Rubell Print Ltd., Bunbury, Tarporley, Cheshire, CW6 9PQ.

Bound by J W Braithwaite and Son Limited, Pountney Street, Wolverhampton WV2 4HY.

CONTENTS

CONTENTS CONTINUED

INTRODUCTION

The first pictures on postcards in this country began to appear in the 1890's and these were quite small, sharing the space of one side with the correspondence. These early picture cards were known as 'Court Cards' and were much smaller than the standard cards of today. Eventually, the size changed and after 1902, one side of a postcard could be used for an illustration, and the reverse side used for correspondence and address. Gradually after this date, postcard collecting became a national craze and postcard albums could be found in a prominent position in almost every home.

Millions of postcards were posted annually, encouraged by the cheap ½d postage rate and the vast output and choice of postcards published, depicting every subject imaginable. This era was known as the Golden Age of Postcards.

The hobby was to remain extremely popular until the end of the First World War, after which it went into a gradual decline, caused mainly by a rise in postage rates and the increased use of the telephone.

During the first twenty years of this century, many postcard publishers were established, which produced a wide range of subject, novelty and view cards. It is to these publishers and photographers that we must be very grateful for recording how things were at the beginning of this century, and also to the families and collectors for saving the postcards; as many would only have been produced in very small numbers.

Chester was very fortunate to have been photographed by many national and local photographers because of its numerous historic sites and photogenic buildings. Many of these postcards depicting Chester have become rare and collectable items.

It is a curious fact that a city famed for its Roman, medieval and Tudor heritage, the Victorian period produced the best known landmarks. The architects mainly responsible for this illusion were Thomas Harrison (1744-1829), James Harrison (1814-66), Thomas M. Penson (1818-64), John Douglas (1829-1911), Thomas M. Lockwood (1830-1900) and W. T. Lockwood (1830-1900). The benevolence and influence of the Grosvenor family is very evident from the use of their name throughout the city.

INTRODUCTION CONTINUED

The sequence of postcards have been selected to follow a tour of the city, commencing with the area inside the Walls, showing details within each quadrant. Then following a tour around the Walls and sampling the delights of the river, before returning to Foregate Street and the east. Finally, the tour ends with a visit to Eaton Hall and the suburbs of Chester.

The postcards also show a selection of local events and transport and illustrate the imperceptible changes that have taken place within the community and to its buildings over a period of forty years.

The pictures are arranged so that it is possible to take this book on the walks and compare present-day Chester with the scenes of earlier times. In addition, closer inspection of the photographs will reveal a wealth of detail.

Postcard collecting has grown in popularity greatly during the last ten years and if you are interested in furthering your knowledge of this fascinating hobby, many societies now exist to assist collectors. Chester has its own postcard club, with meetings held throughout the year at The Peacock Hotel, Christleton Road, Chester on the second Tuesday of every month, commencing at 7.30 p.m.

Finally, we trust this book will bring back many happy memories and give as much pleasure as we have had in selecting the postcards.

Karlyn Goulborn and Gillian Jackson
September, 1987

THE COAT OF ARMS OF CHESTER

The achievement of
Arms was granted in a
charter of 1580.
The left hand side shows the
Arms of England with three
lions passant on a red
background, dimidiated with the
Arms of the Earl of Chester
with three garbs
(golden wheatsheaves)
on a blue background.
The latin motto means
'the ancients look after
the ancient of days'

CHESTER.

HERALDIC SERIES.

1

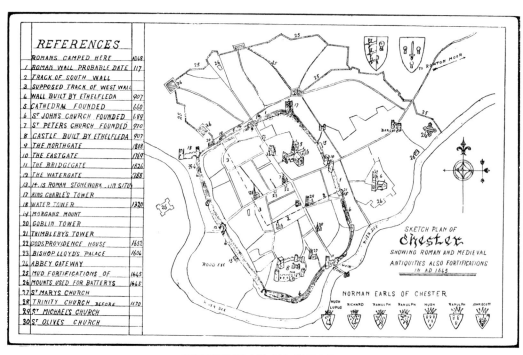

SKETCH PLAN OF CHESTER

This postcard was issued at the beginning of the twentieth century and sold in great numbers.
It shows the city as it was in 1645 during the English Civil War.
The Roman influence is evident from the symmetrical layout of the streets.
The city walls remain much the same today.

THE CROSS, c. 1903
Since Roman times, the Cross has remained the axis of the city.
These famous and much photographed buildings were designed by T. M. Lockwood and
constructed in 1888 by a local company, William Vernon & Sons of
57, Upper Northgate Street, who are still in business today.

Chester

The Cross.

5103 B.

THE CROSS AND EASTGATE STREET, c. 1903

Looking down towards Eastgate Street and showing how the tram lines became a double track
around this corner into Bridge Street.

On the left, at the junction of Northgate Street and Eastgate Street, the postcard shows the
Etonian Economic Clothing Association, which traded here for over sixty years until the late 1960's.

In the right foreground, the small shop was occupied between 1902 and 1933 by Hugo Lang,
a local postcard publisher. After 1933, the premises were taken over by Waltons the Jewellers.

Note the policeman wearing his white pith helment on the left of the picture.

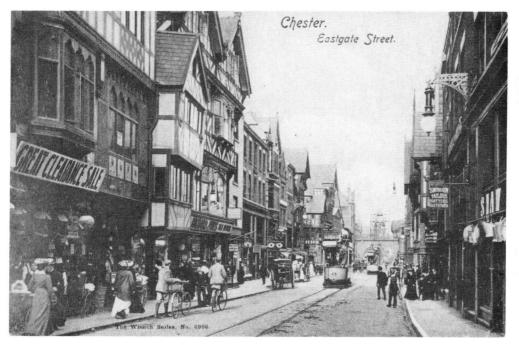

EASTGATE STREET, c. 1905

A busy scene in Eastgate Street! On the left, Cash's bootmakers are holding a 'Great Clearance Sale'. Further along was one of Chester's most popular shops, Richard Jones, the silk mercers, selling clothing and family linens. This building is now occupied by Owen Owen. Richard Jones also had a separate department in Bridge Street for furnishings and funerals.

Above Richard Jones' shop in Eastgate Street were Pullar's dyeworks.

On the right, Shaw's ironmongers have an array of buckets above the shop. Among the services offered in their trade advertisements were the fitting of electric bells and new rollers for mangles!

Eastgate Street, Chester.

EASTGATE STREET, c. 1902

Photographed further along Eastgate Street and approaching the Eastgate.
On the left, the large spectacles belonged to Houghton's, optologist and eyesight specialist.
In addition to selling glasses, they also sold motor goggles!
The premises next door belong to Dutton's, the high-class grocers, who were established in 1854
and had nine separate grocery departments within the shop.
On the right, a horse-drawn dray waits outside J. Little and Sons and a splendid landau collects
or conveys its passengers outside Bollands Restaurant.

EASTGATE ROW, c. 1910

These elaborate carvings front 42, Eastgate Row. The shop was occupied by the booksellers,
Phillipson and Golder, who also sold Chester guide books, stationery and postcards.
The window advertisements read: '3d in the shilling discount off all but net books' and
'Novels published at 6/-, cash price 4/6d'.
The frame on the right shows Ivorex plaster placques of the 'most notable Chester houses'.
These are now collector's items. Looking down Eastgate Row can be seen the entrance to
Bollands Restaurant, before they moved and beyond, Browns of Chester.

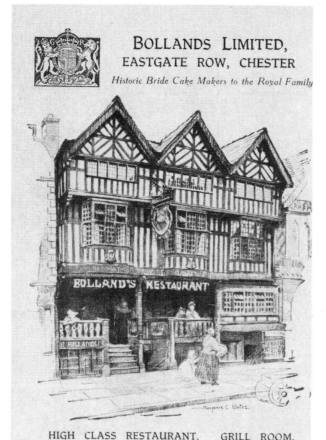

BOLLANDS LIMITED,
EASTGATE ROW, CHESTER

Historic Bride Cake Makers to the Royal Family

HIGH CLASS RESTAURANT.   GRILL ROOM.
(FULLY LICENSED)
LADIES' TEA LOUNGE.   TRIO DAILY.
FINEST CONFECTIONERY.   CHOCOLATES.
TABLE DELICACIES.   .·.   CONTINENTAL COMESTIBLES.

**BOLLANDS LIMITED,
EASTGATE ROW,** c. 1915
Bollands Restaurant occupied the premises at 40, Eastgate Row. When this site was taken over by Brown's department store, this publicity postcard was produced to advertise their new site, which was two doors down towards the Eastgate Clock. Bollands had become famous for having made Queen Victoria's wedding-cake and offered cakes 'as supplied to the Royal Family' from 21/-, which could also be sent abroad packed in tin-lined cases. They also supplied hampers for boating and racing parties. In addition to the restaurant in Eastgate Row, Bollands had a café in the Groves, which was opened during the tourist and summer season.

INTERIOR OF TEA LOUNGE, BOLLANDS RESTAURANT

An evocative and charming scene
from the 1930's, photographed and
produced on a postcard for
Bollands by
Phillipson and Golder Ltd.
The trio played daily between
11 a.m. and 3.30 p.m. for patrons
of Chester's most popular
rendezvous. Motor-cars and cycles
could be parked free of charge,
if dining at the restaurant
and one of the delicacies on their
menu was Turtle Soup, made from
fresh turtles!
The premises were finally sold
in March, 1963.

CORNER OF TEA LOUNGE, BOLLANDS, CHESTER.

9

GROSVENOR HOTEL, EASTGATE STREET, c. 1902

Built on the site of the old Royal Hotel, the Grosvenor Hotel was designed for the Marquis of Westminster in 1863-66 by T. M. Penson. The front of the hotel extends 125 feet along Eastgate Street.
The postcard shown above would have been available free of charge to the guests and used for their correspondence.
The constant clatter of hooves on the granite setts of the street, must have woken many of the guests early in the morning!
J. Little & Sons were family grocers and sited on the corner of Newgate Street, which is now an access to the Grosvenor Shopping Precinct.

THE EASTGATE, c. 1903

The Eastgate was rebuilt in 1769,
replacing an older gate demolished
the year before.
The famous clock, one of Chester's
best-known landmarks,
was given to the city by
Colonel Evans-Lloyd
and erected in a tower of
wrought-iron, which was paid for
using the balance of
Queen Victoria's Jubilee
Celebration Fund.
The clock stands as a memorial
for Queen Victoria's Diamond
Jubilee and was ceremoniously
set in motion by the Mayoress
of Chester on 24th May, 1899
at 12.45 p.m.; the same day as
Queen Victoria's eightieth birthday.
Through the arch can be seen
part of Blossoms Hotel,
before it was aligned with the
rest of the street.

THE EASTGATE, LOOKING TOWARDS
FOREGATE STREET, CHESTER.

11

Eastgate Street, from top of East Gate
Chester.

EASTGATE STREET, c. 1920
Photographed from the top of
Eastgate and looking back along
Eastgate Street towards the Cross,
with the Grosvenor Hotel on the left.
In the foreground, the passing
loop for the trams is clearly visible.
A few horse-drawn vehicles
remain, but motorised traffic is
more in evidence with the owners
having no parking problems!
Also in the right foreground,
the cobbled entrance leads to the
Grosvenor Motor Company.

CHESTER. ST. WERBURGH STREET.

ST. WERBURGH STREET, c. 1905

Formerly St. Werburgh's Lane, the street doubled in width when the fine buildings on the right,
designed by John Douglas, were built between 1895 and 1899.
On the left-hand corner is Parr's Bank, now the National Westminster Bank and on the opposite side
is the Bank of Liverpool, now occupied by Barclays Bank.
Further up on the right of St. Werburgh Street, the arched front belongs to the
Tamil Tea and Oriental Café Company, and next door a display of hats entices shoppers
into Densons, hatters and hosiers.

13

ST. WERBURGH STREET, c. 1920

Looking down towards Eastgate Street and showing the roadway still paved with setts.
On the left, by the bicycle, are the gates leading to Dicksons, the seedsmen, with their name faintly
discernable on the gates. This building is now occupied by a pizza house.
From left to right the businesses include: R. Jones, high class confectionery established in 1880; the Union Bank;
and Chidley's, the photographer and postcard publisher. Mr. Chidley was also the conductor of Chester Glee Club.
Note the man kick-starting his motor-cycle, with its adjoining sidecar.

CHESTER CATHEDRAL, c. 1910

The original building was built on the site of a Saxon church, and became an abbey for the Benedictines in 1092.
Following the dissolution of the monasteries in 1541, the abbey became the Cathedral for the See of Chester.
The gravestones shown in the foreground were removed in 1952 and a Garden of Remembrance laid
out around the Second World War Memorial. The Garden was dedicated on 8th June, 1952.
The Right Reverend Francis Jayne, shown in the inset photograph, was Bishop of Chester from 1889 to 1919.

WAR MEMORIAL, CHESTER CATHEDRAL

Designed by F. H. Crossley and dedicated on 22nd March, 1922. The Memorial cost £760 and was unveiled by Brigadier-General Bromley-Davenport, Lord Lieutenant of Cheshire. The inscription reads:—
"Erected by a Grateful City in memory of her sons, who gave their lives for their country in the GREAT WAR 1914-1918. Their names are engraved on tablets of bronze in The Town Hall and their imperishable memory in the hearts of their fellow citizens."

NORTHGATE STREET, c. 1903

Looking up Northgate Street and photographed just beyond the junction with Eastgate Street.
On the left-hand side of the street can be seen Okell's linen shop, which is holding a Summer Clearance Sale;
Lipton Ltd., the grocers with window posters advertising their prices for cocoa, butter and coffee;
a partial row known as Shoemaker's Row, which was rebuilt in 1897; and at the top,
Densons the drapery store, which fitted an electric lift to service all floors in 1910.
On the right can be seen sides of bacon and ham displayed outside a butcher's shop and the young boy
appears to have been left in charge of the horse and trap, whilst the owners are shopping.

17

CLEMENCE'S CITY CAFÉ & RESTAURANT,
MARKET SQUARE,
TELEPHONE No.
54.
CHESTER.
SPECIAL TERMS & PRIVATE ROOM FOR CHOIR PARTIES, ETC.

CLEMENCE'S CITY CAFÉ AND RESTAURANT, NORTHGATE STREET

Clemence's City Café and Restaurant formed part of a black and white block of buildings that were replaced in the 1960's by a row of modern shops. The postcard shows a grand display of cottage loaves in the right-hand window. Clemence's also used to advertise their special 'artistically decorated wedding-cakes' that could be purchased for one guinea. Concerts were held here every Thursday and Saturday evening between 6.30 p.m. and 11 p.m.

MARKET SQUARE, c. 1925

On the far side of the Square and from left to right, the businesses include: Eastman's, the butchers;
Southard's, the fishmongers with a board outside advertising Turbot at 1/2d per pound;
Milling, the chemist; and Clemences Café and Restaurant.
Sadly all these black and white buildings have been demolished.
On the right of The Square, the public house 'the Dublin Packet' used to be run by the famous footballer,
Dixie Dean. On the corner of Shoemaker's Row is Smith and Sons, the dyers.
Recent pedestrianisation has returned the Square to a traffic free area, but it still remains as busy as ever.

19

WEST FRONT, CHESTER CATHEDRAL, c. 1903
Showing the junction of St. Werburgh Street and Northgate Street.
The building on the left used to house King's School, built in 1878 but founded by Henry VIII in 1541
and originally housed in the Cathedral. In 1904, there were 106 pupils including 14 boarders.
The building is now occupied by Barclays Bank. On the right at the corner of St. Werburgh Street,
was a regular hackney stand, which is just visible in the photograph. At this time, fares for one or two persons
were one shilling for each mile, and sixpence extra for each additional half mile.

THE ABBEY GATEWAY

Adjoining the King's School,
the Abbey Gateway dates back to
the fourteenth century,
with the upper storey being added
c. 1800.
A previous room above the arch
once served as a prison and
George Marsh, the heretic, was
held here before being burnt at
the stake in 1555.
Beyond the gateway in Abbey
Square are the stone houses built
for Bishop Bridgman in 1626.
On the left of the gateway, is
Hewitt's boot and shoemakers,
which is still in business today
as a shoe shop.

ABBEY GATEWAY, CHESTER.

21

Bishops Hostel, Chester.

BISHOP'S HOSTEL, ABBEY SQUARE

Abbey Square was once the site of a section of the monastery, which housed the brewery and bakery. The Bishop's Hostel at number 11, Abbey Square was built in 1784 and formerly the residence of the Dean of Chester.

In 1925, it became the Retreat House under the supervision of three Sisters from the community of St. Peter's, Horbury.

Abbey Square with its splendid Georgian houses can offer a haven of peace in the centre of a bustling city.

Tracks through the cobbles lead right into Abbey Street.

MARKET AND TOWN HALL, CHESTER.

"The Unique Series"

MARKET AND TOWN HALL, c. 1903

One of the greatest losses to Chester's architectural heritage is the baroque frontage of the old Market,
opened in 1863 and demolished in 1967, and now replaced by the soulless Forum.
The Town Hall with its 160 ft. Tower was designed by the Belfast architects, Lanyon, Lymm and Lanyon
and opened by H.R.H. Edward, Prince of Wales in 1869.
It replaced the old Exchange in Northgate Street, which was destroyed by fire in 1862.

TOWN HALL AND MARKET PLACE, CHESTER.

NORTHGATE STREET, c. 1936

The building with the arched windows is Taylor's garage, previously occupied by Lawtons, who, in 1910,
were 'coach builders, harness makers and motor engineers', indicating the transition from horse-drawn to
motor-driven vehicles. It was known as the 'Westminster Coach and Motor-Car Works'
and this title is still visible above the arched windows; the premises now housing the City Library.
To the right is the Shropshire Arms Hotel.

PIED BULL HOTEL, NORTHGATE STREET

This building was originally the Recorder's House and was rebuilt in the 17th century and given a new frontage in the 18th century. It served as a Coaching House and Livery Stables and saw the first Stagecoach service introduced to Birkenhead in 1784.
In 1789, a fire destroyed the stables when a drunken ostler took a candle to bed!
The British travel author, George Henry Borrow (1803-81) stayed here before travelling on to 'Wild Wales'.

The only Original Coaching House in Chester.
(See Sign on Front.)

M. H. HILTON, Proprietor.

25

THE BLUE BELL, NORTHGATE, CHESTER.
LICENSED SINCE 1494.

THE BLUE BELL, NORTHGATE STREET, c. 1926
Parts of the Blue Bell, which is second from right on the postcard, date from the 11th century,
but the building was not licensed until 1494.
This photograph was taken shortly before the Blue Bell closed as an inn in 1930.
It is now a restaurant, despite a previous proposal to ship the entire building to the United States of America.
A. E. Backhouse, Hair Dressing and Shaving Saloon, on the right, has a delightful 'cabin window'
at street level which was added in 1681 and used as a stage coach booking-office.

NORTHGATE STREET, c. 1902

Viewed from the top of Northgate Street and showing on the left: Weighill Brothers, Earthenware Emporium;
the entrance to Abbey Green just beyond; Johns; and in the centre a cycle shop.
On the right of Northgate Street are: the Blue Bell Inn; Backhouse's Hairdressing Saloon, with the barber's
pole protruding at an angle over the pavement; and Davies and Hincks, Agricultural Chemists.
This building became the site of the new Fire Station in 1911 and remained on this site until 1970.
Note the man with his straw hat on his boneshaker bicycle!

CITY WALLS AT THE NORTH GATE, CHESTER.

WATER TOWER STREET, c. 1920

Photographed from the Walls showing a quiet street with the Liverpool Arms on the corner.
Many of the houses have now been demolished for new buildings.
On the right is the Bluecoat School. Beneath the Northgate Arch a poster reads,
"Are you doing all you can to stop Accidents?".

28

Chester Infirmary Extension ... The Duchess ... Memorial Stone York Cook Chester

EXTENSION TO CHESTER INFIRMARY

On 19th September, 1912, the Duchess of Westminster laid the foundation stone of the new Albert Wood wing in Chester Infirmary, which consisted of six pavilion wards. Mr. Wood had generously donated £12,500 to the extension fund. On the right behind the stone, is the architect, Mr. W. Lockwood and to the left of the Duchess, Mr. J. R. Thomson, Chairman of the Board of Management and Dr. Dobie, Hon. Consulting Physician. On the platform are Lord and Lady Grosvenor, Dr. and Mrs. Elliott and Mr. Barbour of Bolesworth Castle, who all made speeches! The wing was officially opened by H.M. King George V on 25th March, 1914. From this date the Infirmary was allowed to use the 'Royal' prefix.

29

WATERGATE AND WATERGATE STREET, p.u. 1905
Watergate was given its name because the tide once flowed to this spot.
The gate was rebuilt in 1788 when the City bought it from the previous keepers, the Stanley family.
From the middle ages, it was the main thoroughfare for Chester's river-borne trade.
When the Dee was canalised in the 1730's, New Crane Street was constructed to link the gate to Crane Wharf.

30

STANLEY PALACE, c. 1900

The Palace was built in 1591
for Sir Peter Warburton,
Member of Parliament for Chester.
It was inherited by his daughter,
who was the wife of
Sir Thomas Stanley,
Controller of the Watergate.
In 1900, the building was in a
fairly delapidated state and
occupied as separate cottages.
It was restored in 1935 and the
Palace is now open to the public.
Access to the Palace is by a narrow
entry from Watergate Street
(shown on the right of the postcard).
The buildings in the right
background abutted the Palace and
were demolished in 1935 to make
way for a fourth gable.

Stanley Palace.

Chester.

Watergate Street.   *Chester.*

The Wrench Series No. 3297.

WATERGATE STREET, c. 1902
This street was once the home to
many affluent families.
The view shows how the street
dips down towards the river.
On the left, the photograph shows
Bishop Lloyd's Palace before
street level improvement and also
note the long striped pole
indicating a barber's shop.
On the right, the outline of the
Holy Trinity Church can be seen.
The Church was rebuilt in 1869
and is now the Guildhall.
Matthew Henry was buried here
even though he was a
non-conformist. (See page 49).

WATERGATE STREET, c. 1900

Looking towards the Cross. The building on the right is 'Uncle Tom's Cabin', which became derelict and later known as 'The Gap'. It has since been replaced by a modern office-block.

A Gazateer dated 1898 gave the following details: "the curious arrangement called the 'Rows'; the front parts of their second stories form a continuous covered gallery, open in front, with private houses above, inferior shops and warehouses below, and the chief shops within."

This view photographed before restoration, illustrates the description very well.

Bishop Lloyds Palace, Chester

BISHOP LLOYD'S PALACE,
c. 1930

The Palace was named after
George Lloyd, Bishop of Chester
between 1605 and 1615,
and was restored by
T. M. Lockwood in c. 1899.
The steps by the young children
in the left foreground, were added
at a later date.
At the beginning of this century,
the Y.W.C.A. was in residence at
Row level and later on, the same
building housed the
Council of Social Welfare.
In the right foreground,
W. E. Speare, Boot and Shoemaker,
advertises 'Nugget' polishes,
shoe repairs, ladies' shoes from
1/9d and gentlemen's shoes
from 2/9d.

YE OLDE LECHE HOUSE

This Tudor dwelling house was probably built c. 1570 by George Leche, 'The Merchant of Chester'. The postcard shows the 'Ladies Bower' (private room) and was used as an advertisement for the House, which was open to the public on weekdays. Today, it is not officially open to the public. Access to the House was through an Antique Shop at Row level, the shop once being the banqueting hall to the House. The building now houses a furniture shop.

COPYRIGHT
CHR. 53

ROWS, WATERGATE STREET, CHESTER,

LILYWHITE LTD.
TRIANGLE, HALIFAX

WATERGATE ROW, c. 1920
Showing Mr. Kenyon's Antique Shop with a fine selection on display at Ye Old Leche House.
A large range of postcards were sold here with views of almost every nook and cranny in the old house
and using sketches by W. R. Boyd.

GOD'S PROVIDENCE HOUSE

c. 1905

Originally built in 1652 and named
in gratitude for escaping the
plague, the house was virtually
rebuilt in 1862.

The premises at street level were
occupied by R. Davies, confectioner,
with a window full of sweet jars
and advertisements for Fry's and
Cadbury's chocolate.

To the right is Quellyn Roberts'
shop and to the left, a butcher's
shop with an open counter and a
selection of fresh poultry and
rabbits hanging above the counter.

The Cross is just visible in the
left background.

God's Providence House
240

Chester. Bridge Street from The Cross.

BRIDGE STREET, c. 1900

The very wide tram tracks were for horse-drawn trams. There is plenty of street activity but little traffic.
The recently completed buildings on the left appear to be empty, with 'To Let' signs in the windows.

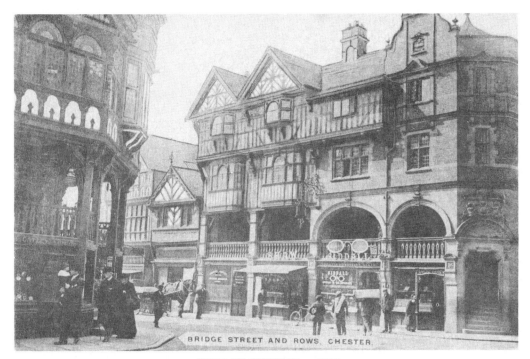

BRIDGE STREET, c. 1905

Viewed from the Cross and looking at the right-hand side of the upper part of Bridge Street.
The shops from right to left are: Donald's chemists, which is now an estate agents; Siddall, optician,
who sold besides spectacles, field and opera glasses, lanterns, slides and oxygen. They also recovered
umbrellas and sunshades 'in all the latest and fashionable colours'! This long-established business is still here
today; Shaw's, ironmongers, who also hired out cutlery and every conceivable type of kitchen utensils;
finally, by the man and horse, is the office of the old weekly newspaper, the 'Chester Courant'.

39

BRIDGE STREET AND ST. PETER'S CHURCH, c. 1903
Looking back towards the junction of Bridge Street and Watergate Street,
where the High Cross has recently been reinstated.
St. Peter's Church was mentioned in the Domesday Book and in the late eighteenth century,
the church buildings were given major alterations.
The Church adjoins the Victoria Dining Rooms, viewed left of centre, and at this time were not licensed.
Above Bridge Street can be seen the recently installed wires for the new electric trams.

ST PETER'S CHURCHYARD,

c. 1932
Photographed at the rear of
St. Peter's Church and the
Victoria Smoke Rooms,
seen on page 40.
The 'Victoria' is licensed and a
painted advertisement on the
back wall reads,
'I always have a Worthington'.
To the left of the Church door
a caged parrot is enjoying
some fresh air!

YE OLDE CRYPTE & CAMPTON HOUSE.   CHESTER.

3827

BRIDGE STREET, c. 1900

The spelling mistake in the title should read Compton House, which is the smaller building in the centre
of the photograph; the shop belonging to the draper, H. Jefferson.
Between Compton House and J. C. and G. R. Brierley, the silk mercers, is Ye Olde Crypte,
which has the oldest crypt in Chester, and at the time was occupied by an ironmongers.
Later it became a café and today, the building is Bookland, the booksellers.
The buildings appear to have been photographed on a hot day as many blinds are in evidence.

42

BRIDGE STREET, c. 1932

Illustrating the notorious bottle-neck that Chester became after the increase in motor traffic!
A fine array of transport is shown on the postcard, including a Cheshire Lines horse-drawn collecting van,
advertising Australian butter, and parked adjacent to Marston's motor stores.
The black and white houses were completed in 1912 to replace a white Doulton Ware facade built in 1910.
This facade was so disliked by The Duke of Westminster that it was immediately pulled down!
The arched windows at street level and St. Michael's Arcade were all that remained.
The angled sign on the right of the picture, belonged to George Barlow, wine merchant.

BRIDGE STREET, c. 1930

Viewed from the centre of Bridge Street and looking back towards the Cross. On the left hand side of the street and from left to right: Davies, motor-cycle dealers, with many advertisements of famous names, B.S.A., Royal Enfield and Sunbeam; S. Allen; The Grotto Hotel; and Barlows, wine merchants.
On the right hand side of the street and from right to left: A. Richardson for 'everything musical'; G. E. Jones, stationer; and Marstons, motor stores, who were able to sell petrol in this busy shopping street. Before Marstons took over the premises, it used to be a Turkish Baths. Tickets were 2/6d in 1912 and ladies were only admitted during two sessions each week.

BRIDGE STREET ROW, c. 1905

This postcard shows the Row before St. Michael's Arcade was built and before
three shops were removed from the Row.
On the left, the smaller building was soon to receive the 'black and white' treatment
and became the Grotto Hotel.
On the right, the window of Richardson's Music Warehouse is full of sheet music and instruments.
In the 1930's, they proudly advertised the 'finest stock of gramophones and records'.

Houses in Bridge Street, Chester

14677

BRIDGE STREET, c. 1905

The alley on the left is Feather's Lane, which once led to the back of a previous building, the Feathers Inn.

The break in the Rows was not bridged until the mid 19th century and in this photograph the smaller central building is occupied at Row level by F. Jones and at Street level by Bennett's, confectioners. On the right is King Charles' House accommodating at Row level Sherratt's Art Gallery and at Street level, W. H. Brazendale, family grocer, tea and coffee salesman, cheese factor and provision merchant.

This shop had many different occupants, many of whom are depicted on contemporary postcards.

BRIDGE STREET, c. 1905
Photographed at the junction
with Pepper Street.
St. Michael's Church, originally a
medieval building was rebuilt in
1849 and closed for worship in
1971. It now serves as the
Chester Heritage Centre.
In the right background in
Pepper Street the almshouses
can be seen, founded in 1658 by
William Jones for four men and
six women.
They were demolished to make
way for the Grosvenor Laing
Shopping Precinct.

57767 ST. MICHAEL'S CHURCH, CHESTER VALENTINES SERIES

47

2, WHITE FRIARS, CHESTER.

WHITE FRIARS, c. 1908
This postcard was probably
published by Mrs. Edge, who ran
'Private Apartments' at
number Two, White Friars,
the entrance being the Georgian
doorway beneath the tall window
(centre left).
Her advertisements at the time
offered 'every attention' in a
'central situation' and located
on the 'General Station to
Saltney tram route'.
The house is now a Solicitor's
office.

WHITE FRIARS, c. 1930
Number one, White Friars
is better known as
Matthew Henry's House,
built in 1658 and the home of the
non-conformist minister in the
late 17th century.
Beyond, on the corner with
Bridge Street, is the rear of the
King's Head Hotel, which has
recently been demolished.

MATTHEW HENRY'S HOUSE, CHESTER.   G.3113.

KING'S HEAD HOTEL, GROSVENOR ST., CHESTER. TEL : 639

PHOTOGRAPH BY SAIDMAN BLACKPOOL

GROSVENOR STREET, c. 1935
Situated at the junction with White Friars, the King's Head Hotel, an early Victorian building,
was allowed to fall into near dereliction and was demolished in 1986.
The site is now being developed as a shopping arcade.
To the right, on the lower wall below the beautifully scrolled and latticed windows
are advertisements for various ales and a Crosville bus time-table.

GROSVENOR STREET, c. 1910

Erroneously titled 'Grosvenor Road' on the postcard. Grosvenor Street was constructed in the early
19th century to connect Bridge Street with the new Grosvenor Bridge.
On the left, the parade of shops include from left to right: a tobacconist;
Simpson's, saddler and harnessmaker; Fred Edge; Joseph Jarvis, florists; and Dodd's Castle Dining Rooms.
On the right from right to left: the red-brick W.R.V.S. building; the junction with Little Cuppin Street;
and a block of buildings, which were demolished for the Inner Ring Road.

Grosvenor Museum, Chester

14703 JV

GROSVENOR STREET, c. 1900
The Museum, designed by
T. M. Lockwood, was opened on
9th August, 1886 by the
Duke of Westminster,
who had donated the land and
£4,000 towards the costs of the
building. At this time,
admission was 3d per person,
but free on Wednesday,
early closing day.
The building on the right used
to be the Chester Savings Bank,
opened in 1853 and which is now
the Trustee Savings Bank.

GROSVENOR SQUARE, c. 1905

Electric tram number Three, about to enter Grosvenor Street, full of passengers from
Saltney and Hough Green.

The clock tower beyond is part of the buildings occupied by the Savings Bank,
and on the right of the photograph can be seen the Castle entrance.

The bronze equestrian statue was modelled by Baron Marochetti and erected in 1879,
in honour of Stapleton Cotton, Viscount Combermere, known as 'the Cheshire Hero'.

Several children are playing around the base of the statue despite the pointed chains!

53

Chester Castle

THE CASTLE, c. 1901

These buildings were based on a competition design won by Thomas Harrison.
They were constructed over several years and completed in 1822.
The left-hand building houses the Military Museum and the centre building was originally the County Hall,
but is now the Crown Court.
Shortly after this picture was taken, a statue of Queen Victoria was erected in Castle Square.
In the foreground, note the wide tracks for the horse-drawn trams.

54

The Castle from River, Chester.

THE CASTLE, c. 1905

Viewed from the river Dee and showing part of the city walls.
In c. 1900, the walls were moved back when Castle Drive was constructed along their former path.
In the foreground above the river bank, the newly planted trees shown in this picture,
now form a leafy avenue along the Little Roodee.
The building below St. Mary's Church tower was the city gaol, which was eventually demolished
to make way for the new County Hall, opened in 1957.

The Bear and Billet, Bridge Gate.   Chester.

The Wrench Series No.11019

THE BRIDGEGATE, c. 1902
Beyond Bridgegate is the Old Dee Bridge with the old Dee Mills, which were demolished in 1910.
The 'Bear and Billet' dates from 1664 and was originally called Bridgegate Tavern,
being the official home of the Sergeants of the Gate.
The upper storey was the family grain store and the folding doors are still there today.

Bear and Billet, and Edgar Tavern, Chester

LOWER BRIDGE STREET, c. 1905

Just above the 'Bear and Billet' and on the corner of Shipgate Street is the Edgar Tavern.
Named after King Edgar, whose palace was in Handbridge c. 973, the Tavern probably dates
from 1500, but was renovated with the additional black and white timber facing in 1895.
At the time this photograph was taken, the Edgar Tavern (Licensee S. Johnson) offered
Refreshment Rooms with 'Accommodation for Cyclists'.
The faint outline of a mounting block can be seen to the right in Shipgate Street.

LOWER BRIDGE STREET, c. 1925

Looking up Lower Bridge Street and on the left, showing number 70, owned by Mr. W. S. Garrad,
who is probably the gentleman standing in the doorway.
Mr. Garrad published this postcard, which is one of a series.
He also sold confectionery and among his signs is one for 'Chester Rock'.
The shop has changed very little over the years, except its name.
The Mons Café painted sign possibly refers to a connection with the Cheshire Regiment.
The Street is cobbled on its left side to assist horse-drawn vehicles up the steep incline from the river.

'CHESTER ROCK'

A novelty 'pull-out' postcard
dating from the 1920's.
The flap was lifted to reveal a
concertina of twelve small
photographs of Chester landmarks.
Could the postcard and Chester
Rock have been sold at
Mr. Garrad's confectionery shop?

SOMETHING SWEET FROM
CHESTER

I'M having quite a Jolly Time,

The Company's good,

the Weather's prime.

And as you'll see from what I send

I'm getting on my "ROCKY" end;

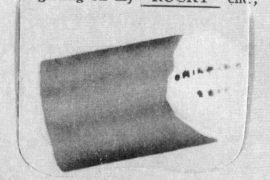

But though I'm busy all day through,

I've time to send some views to you.

1386

OLD HOUSE, LOWER BRIDGE STREET, CHESTER

LOWER BRIDGE STREET,
c. 1902

The 'Tudor House' shown in a very distressed state before its restoration.
Lower Bridge Street had fallen into disrepair when the Grosvenor Bridge opened and Grosvenor Street became the main access road from Wales.
On the left of the 'Tudor House' was a pawnbrokers and the two shops at street level were owned by M. Nolan and A. J. Cartwright, grocer and provision dealer.
On the right, Hawarden Castle Entry led to Albion Street.

LOWER BRIDGE STREET,

c. 1910

Showing the Tudor House after
its restoration, with a much
smarter appearance,
new occupants in the shops and
the pavement properly paved.
On the right, Hawarden Castle
Entry still has an open gutter
running down its length.
The small boy sitting by Quinn's
door is holding a hoop and note
how all the children are fascinated
by the photographer.

THE OLDEST HOUSE, CHESTER.

Chester

Bridge Street.

3317 B.

LOWER BRIDGE STREET, c. 1900
On the corner of Little Cuppin Street, which is now part of the Inner Ring Road, stands the
Falcon Cocoa House. It was originally the Grosvenor's town house, dating from 1626 and restored in the 1880's.
On this postcard, the Falcon is shown as a restaurant with advertising on its windows for
'Teas, Dinners, Chops, Steaks, Pies, Bovril and Billiards'!
The building fell into disrepair and was further restored and re-opened as a public house in 1982.
Further down to the left, 'The White Bear' was a commercial hotel, favoured by Welsh carriers
and beyond are Oddfellows Hall and the Bridge House Club.

PARK STREET, c. 1930

This street runs parallel to the Walls, which are on the left of the photograph.

The facade of the house on the right, bears the date 1881 and the inscription 'The fear of the Lord is a fountain of life', said to be translated from a Roman coin found during excavations on the site.

Beyond are six cottages, part of an original block of nine almshouses, founded in 1658. They were restored in 1969 after becoming derelict and having faced the threat of demolition.

23656. CHESTER. PARK STREET   JUDGES L

63

THE WOLFGATE, c. 1905
This is the oldest remaining gate
of the city and was built in 1760,
with the battlements being added
in 1890.
The Wolfgate was possibly named
after the wolf's head, which was
part of the coat of arms
belonging to Hugh Lupus,
second Earl of Chester,
and had been carved above
the gate.
The buildings adjoining the gate
were in Little John Street and
were demolished when the road
was re-routed and widened in the
1930's.
Through the arch is
Newgate Street.

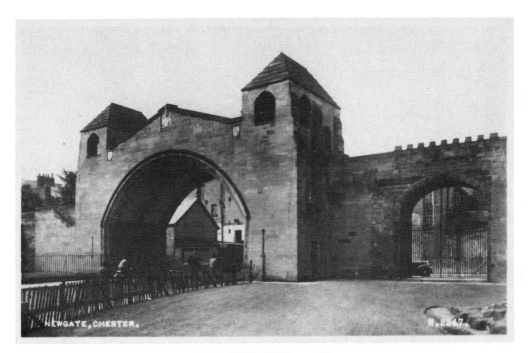

THE NEWGATE, c. 1938

Showing the old Wolfgate with its new neighbour, the Newgate, shortly after its construction in 1937.
Pepper Street is beyond. The buildings visible through the Wolfgate have been demolished and were
in Newgate Street; now the access road for the Grosvenor Shopping Precinct car park.
This is no longer Chester's most recent gate, as St. Martin's Gate dates from 1966,
when the walls were breached near the Royal Infirmary to accommodate the Inner Ring Road.

Cathedral and Walls, Chester

THE CITY WALLS AND CATHEDRAL, c. 1903
The steps on the left lead down to Abbey Street and the Kaleyards Gate.
This was a postern gate allowing the monks to pass from the Abbey to their fields outside the walls.
On the top stone of the left-hand wall is a carving of an anchor with the inscription 692 ft.
This is said to have originated when the British engineer, Isambard Kingdom Brunel (1806-59),
paced the walls from Kings Charles Tower, to determine the length of anchor chain required for the
steamship, the 'Great Eastern', for laying the first trans-Atlantic cable.

THE CITY WALLS AND KING CHARLES' TOWER,

c. 1910

This tower is sometimes called
the Phoenix Tower,
named after the statue beneath
the top arch.
The tower was used as a
Guild Meeting House, with the
phoenix being the emblem of
the Guild of Painters.
King Charles I watched the
Battle of Rowton Moor from here
on 24th September, 1645, before
retiring to the Cathedral tower
to see his army defeated.
On this postcard, the tower is a
private museum, selling souvenirs
and postcards.
It was forbidden to pose for
photographs on the steps!

King Charles Tower,
Chester

KING CHARLES STOOD ON THIS TOWER
SEPTEMBER 24th 1645 AND SAW HIS ARMY
DEFEATED ON ROWTON MOOR.

CHESTER CITY WALL AT NORTHGATE

**THE CITY WALLS AND
THE NORTHGATE,**
c. 1932
The Northgate, designed by
T. Harrison and erected in 1810,
replaced a gate with huge towers
housing the city prison, with
dungeons cut into the rock below.
In 1808, the gaol moved to a site
now occupied by the
Queen's School.
Outside the Walls on the left,
can be seen the Northgate Bakery
and within the Walls on the right,
the building is a café.

THE CITY WALLS AND PEMBERTON'S PARLOUR, c. 1910

Overlooking the Infirmary to the left, Pemberton's Parlour dates from the 13th century and was rebuilt in 1894. Originally a circular tower, twice the height of the present one, it is named after a ropemaker, who used it to oversee his workers below.
Sadly, this rural scene is no more, as the trees were removed to make way for a road.

BONEWALDESTHORNE'S TOWER, c. 1910

Erroneously called the Water Tower on this postcard, it stands at the north-west angle of the Walls and is pictured here from the spur wall linking it to the Water Tower.

The statue of Queen Anne, bearing scorch marks from the fire, which destroyed the Exchange whence it came, has since disappeared.

In Victorian times, a camera obscura was erected on the roof and was a very popular attraction.

THE WATER TOWER, c. 1907
The Water Tower or 'New' Tower
was built in 1322 when the river,
which once reached
Bonewaldesthorne's Tower,
changed its course and a new
tower was needed to protect the
port. The spur wall, linking the
two towers, is clearly seen here
with part of the Water Tower
Gardens to the left.

The Water Tower, Chester (A.D. 1322)

71

Chester, City Walls and Roodee.

THE CITY WALLS, ROODEE AND NUN'S ROAD, c. 1920

On the left of the City Walls is an area known as the Roodee. It was originally a meadow,
previously covered by the river Dee, which reached the Walls at this point. Its name is derived from an
old stone cross or 'rood', which used to stand on an 'eye' or islet in the middle of the river.
In the left background, houses have been built almost to the edge of the race-track,
these were later demolished to make way for new stands.
On the right of the City Walls, the area used to be covered by grass.
It is now Nun's Road, which was laid in 1901, using rubble from the old gaol on the Queen's School site.

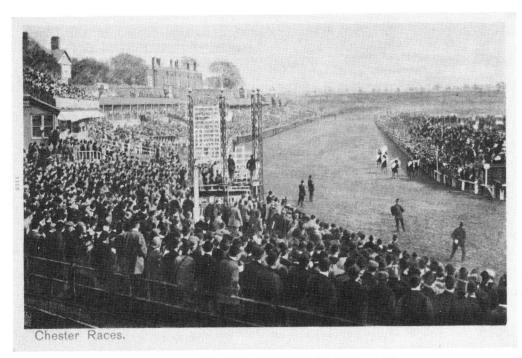

Chester Races.

THE ROODEE AND CHESTER RACES, c. 1903

The 65 acre Roodee has been used for sports since 1540. The Race Company was formed in 1893,
when gate money was also introduced. The Races attract many visitors, including Royalty,
and were always preceded by a grand clean-up of the City!
On this postcard an enormous crowd are enjoying the May meeting, at the time, the only horse-racing event.
The most famous race is the Chester Cup, first run in 1824.

THE CITY WALLS AND EDGAR HOUSE, c. 1910
Showing the City Walls just east of the Bridgegate with the road leading round to the Groves.
The ivy has now been cleared from the Walls.
Edgar House, with the chimneys, was pulled down after the Second World War to be replaced by flats.
The sign on the wall, prohibiting heavy vehicles from this road, is still there today.

S 10293   THE OLD WALLS. CHESTER.

THE CITY WALLS AND RIVER DEE, c. 1905
Photographed from a little further along the Walls and showing the sweep of the river Dee
to the suspension bridge.
To the right on the opposite bank in a very rural setting can be seen the snuff mills of
T. Nicholls and Company. In 1937, Western Command Headquarters were built on the empty field.

River Dee and Suspension Bridge.

THE RIVER DEE AND THE GROVES, c. 1900
The area of the Groves, shown in the foreground, was laid out in the early 1880's by
Alderman Charles Brown, who was one of the 'Browns of Chester'.
The far section towards the Suspension bridge, just visible on this postcard, was still a grassy bank with
a narrow road behind. The bandstand and terrace had yet to be built.

Old Dee Bridge & Mills, Chester.

THE RIVER DEE AND OLD DEE BRIDGE, c. 1902

Once the only crossing of the Dee, this is a medieval bridge with seven arches, no two of which are the same.
Although a footpath was added in 1826, it is still only wide enough for a single line of traffic.
On the Chester side, are the old Mills, demolished in 1910.
In the foreground, is Edgar's Field given by the Duke of Westminster in 1892
to be preserved as an open space.

THE RIVER DEE AND OLD DEE BRIDGE, c. 1925

Viewed from the Groves and looking towards Handbridge, with St. Mary's Church in the background.
This area was the landing stage for the pleasure boats taking passengers up the river Dee.
The sign under the boat's awning reads 'Eccleston Ferry and Eaton Park'.

ECCLESTON FERRY

CHESTER

May. 28th 1903

705 VI

THE RIVER DEE AND ECCLESTON FERRY, c. 1900
Published by Raphael Tuck and showing Eccleston Ferry, a favourite destination for pleasure trips.
There were tea rooms here and frequent boat services, the postcard showing one of the paddle steamers,
which operated from the Groves. Fares were 6d single and 9d return.

The Old Hermitage, Chester.

THE OLD HERMITAGE, c. 1910
This ancient building, also known as the Anchorite's Cell,
is located at the point where Souter's Lane joins the Groves.
Local tradition alleges that it was the retreat of Harold, who was not killed at the Battle of Hastings!
In 1910, the building was owned by the Corporation and used as a Tea House.
It has been moved from its Sandstone base and now has a private house at ground level.

St. John's Church and Landing Stage, Chester.

THE GROVES AND ST. JOHN'S CHURCH, c. 1905
A relaxing day by the river for many Cestrians, showing some about to embark for a steam-boat excursion.
On the left, the large building is the eighteenth century Bishop's Palace,
which became the Y.M.C.A. hostel in 1921.
To the right behind the trees, is St. John's Church, built on the site of a Saxon Church
and was used by the first Bishop of Chester as his Cathedral.

S 3785   SUSPENSION BRIDGE, CHESTER.

THE OLD SUSPENSION BRIDGE, c. 1906
This first bridge was built in 1851 for Mr. Enoch Gerrard, who owned the land on the
Handbridge side of the river. It cost £850, took three months to build and used fifty tons of iron.
It's total length was 417 feet, span 262 feet and it's height above the river 23 feet.
It was strengthened with wire ropes in c. 1893 and demolished in 1922.

The Mayor & Corporation ... over The New Suspension Bridge April 18th 1923 M. Cook City Walls

THE NEW SUSPENSION BRIDGE, 18th April, 1923.
The Mayor and Corporation crossing over the new suspension bridge from the Groves,
at the Opening Ceremony on !8th April, 1923.
The photograph shows the Town Clerk, Mr. J. H. Dickson, wearing his wig and gown, and behind him the
Sheriff, Alderman W. Carr and the Mayor, Mr. Arthur Wall, who officially opened the bridge.
After the opening ceremony and their walk, the official party retired to the Grosvenor Hotel for tea.
The new bridge cost £8,000 and was built to withstand a total weight of 1,200 people.

STUBBS' BOATING Cᵒ Lᵀᴰ
BARGES, BOATS & CANOES FOR SALE OR HIRE
BOATS HOUSED, VARNISHED & REPAIRED
STEAM & ELECTRIC LAUNCHES FOR HIRE
DRESSING ROOMS FOR
LADIES & GENTLEMEN.
REFRESHMENT ROOMS
CYCLES ST

TEA
ROOMS.

THE GROVES, c. 1902

A winter view of the Groves photographed near the bridge and looking towards Grosvenor Park.
A horse-drawn carriage is approaching through the fine avenue of lime trees,
which have now mostly been removed. Stubbs' Boating Co. was one of four boat building firms
situated in this section of the Groves.

Chester Regatta. Racing on the Dee.

CHESTER REGATTA, c. 1902

Still a popular event in the City's calendar today, the Regatta dates from the early nineteenth century.
Spectators gathered along the Long Reach between Earl's Eye and Heron Bridge to watch visiting
rowing club teams compete with the Chester clubs for the City Challenge Cup and other prizes.
The river was illuminated for festivities in the evening.

Grosvenor Monument, Grosvenor Park — Chester

Ankers' Series

GROSVENOR PARK, c. 1905
The twenty acres of land which
became Grosvenor Park,
was given to the Corporation by
the Marquess of Westminster
and opened in 1867.
This splendid statue sculptured
by Thorneycroft was erected by
public subscription in 1869.
The inscription reads:—
"The Generous landlord
The Friend of the Distressed
The Helper of all good works
The Benefactor to this City".

Chester　　　　　　　　　Grosvenor Park in Winter.

5142 B.

GROSVENOR PARK, c. 1903
This view is looking towards the entrance on to Grosvenor Park Road.
The Park was designed by Edward Kemp, a student of Sir Joseph Paxton,
architect of the Crystal Palace, London.

Grosvenor Park Road . CHESTER .

GROSVENOR PARK ROAD, c. 1903
A peaceful scene viewed from the Park Gates. This area is now part of the busy Ring Road.
In the left background, the spire belongs to the Baptist Church and the houses to the right were
designed by Douglas, built in 1880, and look like fairy castles!

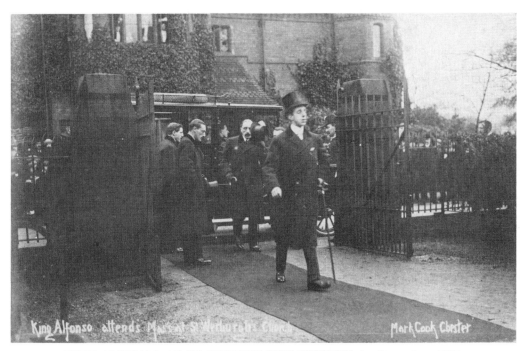

KING ALFONSO AT ST. WERBURGH'S CHURCH, 1st December, 1907.
During His stay at Eaton Hall, the King of Spain and His party attended Mass at St. Werburgh's Catholic Church, in Grosvenor Park Road. He arrived at just before 11 a.m. and walked along a red carpet to the door. The Church was crowded with people, with many having to stand. After a short service, His departure from Church was accompanied by the playing of the Spanish National Anthem.

ST. JOHN'S PRIORY RUINS. CHESTER

ST. JOHN'S RUINS, c. 1910

The church of many towers! In 1468, an old steeple fell in and was rebuilt as a tower
only to fall again in 1572. Two years later, another tower gave way.
The remaining tower stood until 1881 when it also fell, entirely destroying the north porch.
The Duke of Westminster paid for the restoration of the remainder of the church in 1887.

Ursuline Convent, Dee House, Chester

URSULINE CONVENT, c. 1920
The Convent School in St. John Street was opened in 1854.
The Ursulines of Crewe took over the Convent in 1925.
This view of the grounds shows St. John's ruins in the background.
There has been a recent proposal to demolish the school to allow the excavation of the
Roman Amphitheatre, part of which lies beneath the school building.

FOREGATE STREET, c. 1904

Foregate or Forest Street once
formed part of the
Roman Watling Street.
In this superb view taken from
the Eastgate, the Blossoms Hotel
is beyond the National Provincial
Bank on the right, jutting out
onto the pavement, where property
posters are displayed.
Guest and Wardle behind were
cabinet makers, who stocked
"bassinettes and mail carts".
On the left, at no 11, is
Stead & Simpson's Boot Market.
They later took over the adjacent
Hop Pole Café and still trade
from these premises today.

Chester, The Eastgate.

FOREGATE STREET, c. 1905

Looking back to the Eastgate from the corner by Blossoms Hotel,
and showing another Lockwood building on the left.
On the right, a Great Western Railway dray has just collected a keg from
Chester Northgate Brewery's Order Office, now W. H. Smith's shop.
To the far right, Brasseys, ironmongers, with a wall sign pointing to the Post Office
and Free Library in St. John Street opposite.

FOREGATE STREET, c. 1920

The Blossoms Hotel was entirely rebuilt in 1896. The hotel was aligned with Foregate Street and during the alterations was given a new entrance, which was opened in 1911.

The hotel's accommodation also included rooms for the servants of wealthy guests.

The hotel's garage housing thirty cars, was on the opposite side of Foregate Street and can be seen on the far right, on the building with 'Garage' written in vertical letters on the roof.

On the left, the Dee Motor Co. advertises a special show of Rover cars.

FOREGATE STREET, c. 1935

The tramlines have now disappeared, the last tram having run on 15th February, 1930,
making life much easier for the increasing motor traffic.
'Ye Olde Beare's Paw', now Samuel's Jewellers, existed until the 1950's.
On the opposite corner of Frodsham Street, two small shops were demolished and replaced in 1921
by the black and white building, now occupied by the Royal Bank of Scotland.

FRODSHAM STREET, c. 1910

A rare view of the City Arms, built in 1892 at the junction with Union Walk, where on the right, the Stable Block is visible between the trees. It claimed to be "The Cyclists' Home from Home". The postcard shows the staff in the doorway, and was posted in 1910, by the licensee Mr. G. C. Berry, to Wilderspool Ales in Foregate Street – only five minutes walk away! Mr. Berry later took over the Bars Hotel.

Golden Lion Hotel. Mrs. Watkins, Foregate, Chester.

FOREGATE STREET, c. 1904
Returning to Foregate Street, and showing the Golden Lion Hotel. The Watkins family were licensees
from 1876 to 1917, when W. J. Milton took over. He changed its use to a garage in 1929.
The alleyway on the left, led to the stables and looseboxes.
In 1932, Marks and Spencer acquired the site for their Department Store.
On the right, note the carcasses of meat hanging outside the butcher's shop belonging to W. and H. Williams.

FOREGATE STREET THE OLD NAGS HEAD HOTEL CHESTER

FOREGATE STREET, c. 1915
The Old Nag's Head was rebuilt
in 1914 and restored in 1980 to
become, with the block to its right,
Boots the Chemist.
The wrought iron bracket for the
Hotel sign still remains today.
Their garage could accommodate
twenty five cars with parking
charged at 6d for all day!
This was also the departure point
for conveyances to Kelsall and
Tarvin.

Foregate Street, Chester.

FOREGATE STREET, c. 1925

In the centre of the postcard, the circular sign belongs to number 73, The Globe Boot and Shoe Company.
From left to right the other businesses include: The Imperial Studio; a picture framers;
the White Lion public house, which ceased to be licensed in 1931; and on the far right,
Richardson's Glass, China and Fancy Bazaar having a tempting array of souvenirs and pottery.
This shop is now a furniture showroom.

THE BARS HOTEL, FOREGATE STREET, c. 1915

Chester has no natural defences on its eastern boundary;
this resulted in the city being protected by a Wall, which remained until 1770.
The wall included an arch and postern gate, from which the 'Bars' Hotel takes its name.
George Berry, formerly of the City Arms, became the licensee in 1911 and, with his apparent love for
postcards, produced this advertising card showing a superb line-up of motor-cars posed for the camera.
On the reverse of the postcard, the hotel gives details of its garage with accommodation for over 100 cars
and the hotel telephone number, Chester 4.

CITY ROAD, c. 1906
Before City Road was built in the 1860's, a footpath led across the fields from the station,
which had its main approach via Brook Street.
Looking up the right-hand side of City Road can be seen the Royalty Theatre.
The spire in the distance belongs to the Wesleyan Methodist Chapel.
This area, at the junction with Foregate Street, has changed considerably
following the building of the city ring road.

THE STAFFORD HOTEL, CITY ROAD, c. 1922

The hotel was formed in the early 1920's, from a block of three separate houses at 39, 41 and 43 City Road,
as is apparent from the three entrances.
The 'Stafford' was a temperance hotel and one of a multitude of hotels, restaurants and cafés
catering for travellers arriving in the city by train.
To the left, City Road rises to cross the canal.

THE "WESTMINSTER HOTEL." CHESTER.

W. H. ANKERS, PHOTO. CHESTER.

THE WESTMINSTER HOTEL, CITY ROAD, c. 1903
Another of the splendid large hotels situated along City Road.
To the left is the corner of Tramway Street, which led to the Tram depot
and now the City Corporation bus terminus.
A collection of carter's vehicles can be seen at the side of the hotel,
with the tram sheds just visible beyond.

**ELECTRIC TRAM AT THE
STATION TERMINUS,**
c. 1905
A rare and very collectable
postcard showing the Number 5
electric tram owned by
Chester Corporation Tramways,
with its driver and conductor
posing for the photographer
outside the Queen Commercial
or Albion Hotel and with the
Station tower in the background.
The Electric trams first ran in
Chester in 1903; the colour of
their livery being apple green
and ivory.

QUEEN HOTEL. CHESTER

LODGE, PHOTO
CHESTER

QUEEN HOTEL, CITY ROAD
The hotel faces the station at the end of City Road, and stood opposite the old 'Albion' (1867)
or 'Queen Commercial' hotel, which is now the 'Town Crier'.
It was built in 1860 and had to be rebuilt a year later when it was seriously damaged by fire.
There was a covered walk to the station platforms and the hotel porters dressed in scarlet livery,
met all the trains.
The hotel had its own telegraph office and was linked to the Albion Hotel by an underground passage.

ST. PAUL'S CHURCH, BOUGHTON, c. 1905

St. Paul's Church was built in 1830, renovated by Douglas in 1876 and features some stained glass by
Burne-Jones. The Church overhangs the riverbank and because of its orientation, the chancel faces south.
On the left, next to the Church is the Campbell Memorial Hall, designed by Lockwood, and
erected in memory of the Reverend E. A. Pitcairn-Campbell, by his widow.
On the right, the roof-tops belong to the houses on Barrel Well Hill,
which used to be the site of many executions.

106

BOUGHTON POST OFFICE, c. 1904

Travelling between Christlon Road and St. Werburgh Street, a number 5 tram has stopped at the junction,
where Boughton divides into Tarvin Road on the left and Christleton Road on the right.
Many empty seats are visible on the tram, perhaps the group of people were about to board the tram
when the photographer had finished!
On the extreme left, the tram 'stop' is compulsory. It was coloured red and white and read
'All cars stop here'. Request stops were coloured blue and white.
The Post Office, in the centre, was designed by Douglas and is now a model shop.

Flookersbrook Hoole. CHESTER.

FLOOKERSBROOK, HOOLE, c. 1903

Flookersbrook takes its name from the stream, which runs across the land behind the railway station.
In the middle of the eighteenth century, houses were built on this land for the railway workers.
On the left on the corner of Ermine Road, is the Ermine Hotel and livery stables and left of centre,
the shop belongs to T. Carter, Chemist and Post Office.
The area's main claim to fame is that during the English Civil War, Parliamentary forces camped here
throughout the four month siege of Chester in 1645.

HOOLE ROAD, c. 1905
Recent completion of the M53 has turned this peaceful road into a busy thoroughfare.
In contrast to terraced houses nearer the railway, this road is lined with large villas,
many of which have been converted into flats, hotels and guest houses.
During the tram era, a service was planned to run from the station along Hoole Road,
but it was never achieved.

UPTON CHURCH, c. 1903
Just along Church Lane is the Church of the Holy Ascension,
another building designed by James Harrison.
It was built of local red sandstone in 1854, to serve the needs of the growing village of Upton
which has now become a thriving suburb of Chester.

110

THE GROSVENOR BRIDGE, c. 1912

A distant view from the Dingle with the Roodee in the centre.
The Grosvenor Bridge was built to provide better access from the south and Eaton estates.
The foundation stone was laid by Earl Grosvenor in 1826 and the bridge opened by Princess Victoria
in 1832 even though it was unfinished!
The span is 200 feet and at the time, was the largest single span in the world.
It was a toll bridge until 1885.

HOUGH GREEN, c. 1905

A knife-grinder plies his trade on the road to Saltney and North Wales.
The horse-drawn trams travelled along this road from 1879, and on the right,
an electric tram makes its return journey.
Above the tram-driver, the advertisement reads, 'Richard Jones for Drapery and Furniture'.
In the city centre all the trampoles were fitted with street lights, but beyond the Grosvenor bridge
and in this area, the lights were fitted on every fourth pole.

OVERLEIGH LODGE, c. 1903

The Lodge and Gates are sited at the end of what was the main Chester approach to Eaton Hall.
Locally called "Duke's Drive", it is now a favourite walk for Cestrians on Sunday afternoons.
The Lodge was built in the 1890's and designed by R. W. Edis.

S 3788   THE GOLDEN GATES, EATON HALL, CHESTER.

EATON HALL, c. 1910

The Golden Gates, the main entrance to Eaton Hall, date from the eighteenth century when the first Hall
occupied this site. The railings swept back from the gates, forming a semi-circular courtyard.
When the third hall was built, the architect, Waterhouse, straightened the railings and extended them
to include small gate-houses and a wall to enclose the gardens.

EATON HALL, c. 1910

This is the third of four houses built on this site for the Grosvenor family, each incorporating parts of the earlier houses, the first being built in 1675.

Designed by Alfred Waterhouse, this Gothic Hall with its chapel and tower was begun in 1870 and took twelve years to complete. The clock tower has twenty eight bells, the largest weighing two and a half tons, which play forty eight tunes, including "Home Sweet Home", to greet the Duke on his return to the Hall.

Eaton Hall.

EATON HALL, c. 1902

From the East Front, the terraced gardens sweep down to the river.
The Grosvenors employed the best landscape gardeners of the period, including, Capability Brown,
William Webb and Sir Edward Lutyens, to create the magnificent park.
The main block of the Hall is on the left, with the private appartments to the right.
The Hall was demolished in the 1960's with the exception of the chapel, tower and stables.

EATON HALL GARDENS,

c. 1910

The Aviary was one of many ornaments in the grounds. This circular building serving as the parrot house was designed by Waterhouse in the style of classical Greek architecture, supported and surrounded by Ionic pillars.

THE AVIARY,
EATON HALL GARDENS.

W. H. ANKERS, PHOTO, CHESTER.

117

LIZZIE CASWALL SMITH.

905 A   THE DUKE OF WESTMINSTER   ROTARY PHOTO. E.C.

THE DUKE OF WESTMINSTER

The Grosvenors have been
Earls of Chester since the
time of William the Conqueror.
The Eaton Estate has belonged
to the family since the fifteenth
century.
Hugh Lupus Grosvenor, 1827-1899,
was created the first Duke of
Westminster in 1874.
The second Duke, Hugh Richard
Arthur Grosvenor, 1879-1953,
was his grandson, shown on this
postcard aged about eighteen
and in his final year at Eton.

MR. R. A. YERBURGH, M.P.

Robert Armstrong Yerburgh
was born in 1853, in Sleaford,
Lincolnshire.
Educated at Harrow and Oxford,
he was Conservative Member of
Parliament for Chester from
1886 to 1906 and 1910 to 1916,
in which year he died.
During his time in Chester, he
was President or Vice-President
of most of the city's sporting
clubs and was involved in the
Chester Pageant of 1910.

MR. R. A. YERBURGH.

Wish I could "A Ford"
Another Week at CHESTER

Packed underneath this Ford you'll see
Some views to show I think of Thee.
1415

'ANOTHER WEEK AT CHESTER'
A comic card of the mid 1920's and a tribute to the growing popularity of the 'affordable' Ford motor-cars.
The flap on the front lifts up to reveal a concertina of 12 small views of the city.

National Publishers of Chester Postcards

Blum & Degan
Boots, Pelham Series
Brown & Rawcliffe

E. T. W. Dennis, Scarborough

Excel Series

C. W. Faulkner & Co.
Friths

Gottschalk, Dreyfus & Davis

Hartmann

Jackson & Son, Grimsby
Judges

Knight Collection

Lilywhite Ltd.

Misch & Stock

Palatine Pictorial Co. Ltd., Manchester
Pictorial Postcard Co. Ltd.
Pictorial Stationery Co. Ltd.

Radermacher Aldous
Rapid Photo Printing Co. Ltd.
W. Ritchie & Sons
Rock Bros. Ltd.
Rotary Photo

Walter Scott, Bradford
Shureys Publications
W. H. Smith & Son

A. & G. Taylor
Raphael Tuck

Valentines
Charles Voisey

J. Welsh & Sons
Woolstone Bros.
Wrench

Local Publishers of Chester Postcards (based in Chester)

W. H. Ankers

T. Chidley
Mark Cook

W. S. Garrad
R. Green of Saltney

Huke's Library
Hyde's Series

Hugo Lang
C. H. Lodge

Phillipson & Golder

F. Richardson
Will R. Rose

Archer Smith
Thomas Swift

ACKNOWLEDGEMENTS

All the postcards featured in this book have been selected from the author's collections.
Cover Design: based on original artwork by Sally Mancell.
Editorial: Steve Benz.

Also published by S. B. Publications:—
Chesterfield: A Portrait in Old Picture Postcards
Bootle: A Portrait in Old Picture Postcards